STORY OF BALANCE SHEET

Written By

J.P. Indora

Controller of Finance & Accounts

Disclaimer

It is purely a work of fiction to make understand the Accounting System. Any resemblance to any name or Person may be coincidence only, not for the purpose of causing hurt or harm to any person.

J.P. Indora

The Background

- Mohan Lal joined one of premier institute of Government situated at Delhi on 18.01.1997 as Section Officer (F&A) . For him, Balance Sheet was somewhat tough subject in the initial stage as he was not from the background of

- Commerce. Usually he used to visit one of the Big temple at Delhi where one of his best friend Mr. Sohan Lal was one of the Accounts Officers in the Satsang. He (Mohan) learnt the concepts of Balance Sheet from him (Sohan Lal) in June, 1998.

- W.e.f. 01.04.2003, New Accounting System on Accrual Basis was introduced in his department. Mohan Lal was somewhat confused regarding Accrual System. On 31st March, 2004, Mohan Lal visited the temple to meet his friend to take some knowledge on the closings of the Accounts so that proper Balance Sheet could be prepared for 2003-2004.

- He told him (Sohan) his (Mohan) problem about accrual accounting and about Balance Sheet of 2003-04 to be prepared after closing.
- Mohan:- Yaar, I am unable to understand this accounting system on Accrual basis.
- Sohan:- You show me your Balance Sheet of 2002-03.
- Mohan:- Ok, I show you.
- Sohan:- It is very simple.

- (Sohan takes him to the backside of the Satsang and from here Story of Balance Sheet starts).
- Sohan:- See this building and look at these three Daanpatras i.e. One very big and two smaller than this. This temple is controlled by the Government. One of the Government Department comes here every year after start of financial year and put crores of Rupees in the Big Daanpatra. Shardhalus

also come and give money in Big Daanpatra. 75% of Ashirwad money also goes to Big daanpatra. 25% of Ashirwad money goes to second daanpatra. The mundan ceremony is also performed in the temple and the fees taken for this purpose also goes in the second daanpatra and so on.

Being controlled by the Government, Our temple has

give receipt for the each penny we receive from the Government or Shardalus. Each and every transaction (Receipt/Payment) are recorded in the relevant registers without fail. Our Accounts are Audited by the State Government agency, every year.

(Near Daanpatras, some Parvachan is being given by some Baba)

- Mohan (Seeing the Baba):- I see he is Baba

Dharam Pal who is giving parvachan to Shardalus. There are queues of shardalus who are depositing the money. Do you people take money from shardhalus who come here to take Ashirwad from Baba Dharam Pal who is said to be privileged to receive Antargyan from some Goddess.

(They move further and go near Queues)

- Sohan:-Mohan, I have forgotten to tell you one thing.
- Mohan:-What is that?
- Sohan:- We have used Big ATM Machines through which the amount goes in Daanpatras, hence automatic calculation of money deposited in all the three Daanpatras. We also use Big ATM Machine at the main window of Daanpatras through which money is withdrawn and Small ATM Machines at the doors of Building No. 14, 13, 12, 8, 6 and 5 which automatic count the amount dispersed through each of them.

- Sohan(further tells):- On 31st March of each year we close all the windows of Daanpatra except window no. 8. The balance amount in each Daanpatra as on 31st March comes out through this window and automatic calculated and it is the Closing Balance on 31st march and It is depicted in Register No.8 as "Balance in Daanpatra". It is pertinent to mention here that the same amount will be again put in three Daanpatras as per their Balances and it will be treated as Opening Balance for the next financial year.

- Sohan (further tells):-All the three Daanpatras are like a Big Petrol Pump where Petrol, CNG and Diesal are dealt with. The Petrol, CNG and Diesal are stored in Big Tanks and through out the year all these three items are continuously supplied to the Tanks and from these tanks Petrol, CNG and Diesel are supplied to various vehicles like Bikes, Cars, Tractors, Trucks and many more vehicles through the Machines which calculate the supply of these three commodities. On 31st March of each year , the total supply in the Big Tanks and total consumption through out the year and Balance quantity is checked.

- In this way , total receipt ,total consumption and Balance is ascertained. It is like your Receipt & Payment account and it has no concern with Income and Expenditure. Whatever goes in and whatever comes out is "Receipt and Payment Account)
- (Now they move further to see the queues which were there and people were depositing the money).

Last Year Ashirwad taken Deposit Window (D)	Current year Ashirwad Deposit Window (R)	Next year Ashirwad Deposit Window (T)/Pre-paid receipt/Adv.receipt

- Sohan (Replies to Mohan):-Yes, the Shardalus buy tickets to attend Satsang. Tickets are also given on credit basis (Udhaar Basis) as our Shardalus are very honest person and also loyal to Baba ji. Baba ji has full faith in his Shardalus. Last year on 31.03.2003, Baba ji gave Ashirwad to Shardalus. Some shardalus could not pay on 31.03.2003 and after that Baba Ji was out of country and now he has come and they are paying now in this current financial year 2003-04.

In Ist Queue on 'D' Window, we are taking money for the Ashirwad provided on 31.03.2003 in the last financial year; In the second queue at window 'R' we are taking the money for this Ashirwad Satsang which is going on for the last 10 days; In the third queue at window 'T' we are taking advance payments for the Satsang to be held in next F. Year in June, 2004 for one month.(Lets move further where payments are being made)

Last Year Outstanding Expenditure Payment Window (S)	Current year Expenditure Window (P)	Pre-paid Expenses Window (E)

- Mohan (Further):- See, some people are taking the money from DaanPatra at window 'S' and some are at window 'P' and some are from window 'E' and getting it entered in the registers. Why is it so?
- Sohan:- At window 'S' the vendors are taking their payments which was not paid till 31.03.2003 although payable in f.y. 2002-03. At window 'P', the employees are taking money from Daanpatra to purchase AATA,

CHAWAL, DAAL etc. for Bhandara as well as for Stock purpose to be kept in central stores. They are also taking money for purchase of One Mercedes car for Baba ji and for some other equipments, computers, furniture etc.

- Mohan:- I think you make all expenditure (Revenue/Capital) from these three Dhanpatras?

- Sohan:- Yes. We make most of the expenditure from the Big Daanpatra and if sometimes there is lack of money in this Dhanpatra, we make expenditure from the Second Daanpatra. Third one is for outside parties only and expenditure is met from this Daanpatra for their own works only. Receipts in Daanpatras and Payments from them are like your 'Receipt and Payment Account'. All money comes in and goes out through these DaanPatras only.

- Mohan:- Ok, now I understood what is R&P Account. Please tell how you people record detailed transactions of Reccipts and Payments.
- (Sohan takes Mohan further where there are Two Blocks i.e. Revenue Block (Block-A) from Building No. 14 to 9 and one unnumbered building for calculations of Income and Expenditure during and on the closing of the year; Capital / Asset Block (Block B) from building no. 8 to 6;

5 is Liability Calculation Building; The Reserve Block in Building no. 2; Capital Fund Building No. 1 and Balance of Liability & Asset Building without no.).

- Mohan:- Ok. Lets go there in each building one by one.
- Sohan (Taking him to each building one by one):- Look, this is Laboratory (Building No. 14) and lots of chemical, Consumables

and other related items are kept here to prepare sanitizer to kill insects. We purchase them from the market. Approximately Rs.4.00 Crore are used annually for this purpose. We use Register no. 14 to enter the expenditure transactions. This amount comes from Daanpatra-1 and sometimes from Daanpatra-2.

- Mohan:- Ok. It is like our Schedule 14.

- Sohan:-Yes.
- Sohan:- Please look at building no. 13. Electricity bills are being paid here and the building is also got repaired. We also make other Administrative Expenses on Electricity, Maintenance of Buildings, Colony maintenance, contingencies and on many other items to maintain the Temple properly. This expenditure is recorded in Register No. 13.

- Mohan:- I think it is like our Schedule 13. It is the expenditure like our P-04, P-06, P-701 and alike.
- Sohan:-Yes.
- (Sohan takes his friend Mohan further)
- Mohan:- Yaar, there is much crowd in Building no. 12. What this crowd is about?
- Sohan:- Some employees are being paid medical bill payments, TF, Bonus,

OTA, Hon., LTC payments etc. These payments are recorded in register no. 12. Through out the year except March salary, salary to all the employees has been paid through this window only.

- Mohan:- Ok, it is like our schedule 12 .
- Sohan:-Yes.

(They move further and they see some more queues of people in another section i.e. Receipt section).

Income Window 11('R') Employees	Income Window 11 ('R') Employees & Others

- Mohan:- Please see building no. 11 where people are standing in the rows. What are these rows?
- Sohan:-Some empty drums are being sold there and people are depositing the purchase money. In second line people are depositing Licence Fees for their quarters and for some other misc. works. These receipts are recorded in Register no. 11.
- Mohan:- Ohh! It is like our schedule 11. (They move further and they further see two Queues)

Income Window 10('R') Bank Officials	Income Window 10 ('R') Employees

- Mohan:-Why there is crowd in building no. 10?
- Sohan:- In first line, these are officers from the Banks who are depositing the Interest Amount on term deposits, on saving account and interest on margin money etc due upto February 2004. The next interest will be deposited by them on 30.04.2004. In the second line, employees are depositing interest on loans like HBA, PC and Conveyance etc. due upto 31.03.2004 i.e. in this

financial year only. These receipts are recorded in Register no. 10.

- Mohan:- It is like our Schedule 10.
- Mohan:- For what purpose this Building No. 9 is?
- Sohan:- Our Accounts Officer dealing with revenue expenditure sits in this building and now he is calculating how much money has been utilized on Revenue

Account from Government grand(Daanpatra-1) and from Reserves (Daanpatra-2). It is pertinent to mention here that Daanpatras are kept in a Building in between building no.14 & 8 before Block-A and Block-B starts. In Block-A, from Building No. 14 to building No.9, the Register no. 14 to 12 for Revenue Expenditure and Register No. 11 to 9 for Revenue Receipts, are maintained properly.

- The register No. 9 is meant for the records how much money has been utilized from the money given by the Government in big Daanpatra-1 and how much money has been utilized from the Second Daanpatra-2 etc.

- Mohan:- Ohh! It is like our schedule 9 and thc first Daanpatra is like money in the form of Govt. GRANTS and Second Daanpatra is like Reserve Fund.

- Sohan:-Now next building is there where another Accounts Officer sits to calculate the total expenditure from the Register No. 14 to 12 and total revenue receipts from the register no. 11 to 9. The figures of Increase/Decrease of Inventories are also recorded here being income. The figures of Depreciation as per Register 6 are also recorded being loss. We call this Register "Income and Expenditure Statement".

- The Accounts Officer fills the figures of income and expenditure from register no. 11 to 9 and 14 to 12 respectively in the Register of Income and Expenditure. Loss on account of Depreciation is also accounted for in this register as Expenditure, the entry taken from Register no. 6. Increase/Decrease of Inventories is also accounted for in this register as Income, the entry taken from Rcgister no. 8.

- The total figure of expenditure is subtracted from the total figure of Income. If the figure of Income is more than the Expenditure, the figure is shown under "Balance being excess of Income over Expenditure" and If the figure of Income is less than the Expenditure, the figure is shown under "Balance being excess of expenditure over Income" and figure also goes in Capital Fund Register No. 1.

- Mohan:- It is also like our Income and Expenditure Account.
- Sohan:-Yes.
- Mohan:- I think this Block-A of Revenue Expenditure & Revenue Receipt after Income and Expenditure Statement building comes to end here. Where to go now?

Accrued Income ('I') Window	Outstanding Expenditure Window ('O')

- Sohan (Giving Sign to two Queues):- Please see the Queues at thc start of Capital Block. These are very important windows for Accrual system. Now we will go to Capital Block which is in another line of buildings i.e Block-B.
- Mohan:- Ok.

- Sohan:- See this is building no.8 and all records are maintained in register no. 8. All the transactions relating to Current Assets including Stock Inventories purchased from revenue heads and are lying in stock of Central Stores which is adjacent to this building no. 8; Cash & Bank Balance; Advances to employees (Both interest bearing and non-interest bearing); pre-paid advances; Accrued Income;

advances and other recoverable payments; excess expenditure on external projects; advances for ECF; Recoupment due-PF and others etc; are recorded in Register no. 8.

- Mohan:- It is like our schedule no. 8.
- Sohan:-Yes.
- Mohan:- What is this building no. 6? It is very big building.
- Sohan:- Our fixed Assets purchased out of capital

grant like Apparatus & Equipments, Workshop Machinery, Computer Equipment/Major Computer software, Office equipments, furniture & fittings, Model & Exhibits, Vehicle and Transport, Tools & Plants, Electrical installations and equipment, Library books etc. are placed in this building and the transactions are recorded in Register no. 6. The other transactions like

- Work-in-progress and electronic journals are also recorded in this register.
- Mohan:-Sohan, the date of purchase and amount of purchase has been mentioned on all the items placed in building no. 6 and on most of the items year wise amount of depreciation and net value in reducing way has been mentioned. Some new Cars are also standing in the building but no amount of

depreciation has been mentioned on them. Why all these amounts are mentioned on the items?

- Sohan:- Mohan come here and sit in the car. I will show you something. See, all the copies of year wise insurances of the car. In the year of purchase of car, the value of car has been shown as full value of Car. In the next year, value of car has been somewhat reduced. In the second year, the value is further reduced and so on. It is the 15th year of this car and the value has been mention as Rs. ONE only. The life span of car has been fixed by the Government at 15 years only.

- The value of this car has been continuously reduced in the insurance policy. Reduction of the value of car year to year is Depreciation charged. Now this car has been sold in Auction to a

Kabari for Rs. 25001/-. In this way , the profit of Rs. 25000/- has been occurred and this profit of Rs. 25000/- will be accounted for in Register no.11 under the head "Profit on sale of Assets". The asset will be written off from the register no. 6 through C-Voucher and the residuary value of car i.e. value of Rs.1. It will be recorded in Register no. 13 under the head "Assets written off".

- Like this transaction, other items are also depreciated keeping in view their life span and loss on account of written off of Asset is accounted for in register no. 13 and sale value of written off Assets will be accounted for in Register no.11 under the head "Profit on sale of Assets". The land and Buildings on which this temple is situated are also accounted for in register no. 6.

- Mohan:- Now, I understood what is our schedule-6 (Fixed Assets). Now I understood why different percentage of depreciation has been fixed for different items in schedule-6. Each type of item has its own life span and accordingly the percentage of depreciation has been fixed.
- Mohan:- Who are there in building no. 5?

- Sohan:- Lets visit building no. 5 and you will yourself know who they are.
- Sohan:- They are the persons who had given the amount in Big Daanpatra, Second Daanpatra and 3rd Daanpatra. They are here to know the status of their money i.e. How much is balance. They are Lendaar (Creditors). In addition to them, therc are officials from other departments like Income

- Tax etc. to take I.tax yet to be paid by the temple.
- Mohan:- There are none in building no. 4 and 3. These are empty. What about next?
- Sohan:- Now we will visit building no. 2 where Accounts Officer is checking the transactions of money in Register no. 2. He is checking how much amount was generated during the year in this second Daanpatra and how much was utilized on Capital account and Revenue

Account. He is checking how much is balance in the Second Daanpatra and Register no. 2. After ascertaining the correctness of the amount he will move the balance in Balance Sheet.

- Mohan:- Ok, now I understood about register no. 2. It is like our schedule 2 (LRF). What next?
- Sohan:-Next is Building no. 1. All the transactions are recorded in Register no. 1. It is called Capital

Fund. All the transactions related to capital expenditure are recorded in this register no. 1. Even balance in the form of Cash or Kind from Income and Expenditure Account is recorded here. The total of Capital Fund is carried to Balance Sheet of the year under Liabilities Head.

- Mohan:- Ok, now I understand. What is next?

- Sohan:- Now it is the register of Balance Sheet called Balance Sheet itself. The totals of Register No. 1, 2 and 5 are recorded under the head "Liabilities" under different headings and the totals of Register No. 6, 7 & 8 are recorded under the different heads of Asset side of Balance Sheet. If Difference of Asset and Liabilities is "NIL", then Balance Sheet is OK.

- (Now, Mohan was having the perfect knowledge of what was Balance Sheet and Mohan continued to prepare the proper Balance Sheet upto 2022-2023. There is Accrued Income and also Outstanding Expenses for the F.Y. 2022-23 which are being entered in the proper registers (As per the Queue in next page) which will be received/paid during 2023-24.

Accrued Income ('I') Window	Outstanding Expenditure Window ('O')

- Sohan:- In first line, these are officers from the Banks who are giving the figures of the Interest Amount on term deposits, on saving account and interest on margin money etc due as on 31.03.2004, not actual payment. In the second line, the employees are standing only to get their salary slip to know the amount of their salary which is although due on 31.03.2004 but it will be disbursed on 01.04.2004 or on later date.

- (Now Sohan is clarifying many salient features to Mohan through the actual activities)
- The pictures of activities which are being done on dated 31.03.2004
- 1. Shardalus and others are depositing the money in Daanpatras and getting the money receipts which will be accounted for in different registers as mentioned in the Story. Unauthorized deposit in Daanpatra is not allowed. Bank

account of the temple is not disclosed to anyone like departmental account of some of the Departments who only authorise some of the branches of Banks to take cheques/DDs on their behalf.

- 2. Money is being dispensed off from Daanpatra-1 and sometimes from Daanpatra-2 through the taps, for the expenditure (Revenue & Capital) by the officials in Building No. 14,13,12,8,7,6 etc. to pay to the employees as well as to the private parties.

- 3. In First Block, presently there are seven Buildings (Left to Right) i.e. Building No. 14,13,12,11,10,9 and one last building without number.
- 4. In the second Block also, presently there are seven buildings (Left to Right) i.e. Building No.

- 8,7,6,5,2,1 and One without number. In Building no. 5, the transactions (Receipts & Expenditure) of Daanpatra-3 are accounted far.
- 5. It is informed that Building in which Income and Expenditure Statement is being prepared, is without number as there are no receipts or expenditure from this building and is last in the Block.

- 6. It is informed that Building in which Balance Statement is being prepared, is without number as there are no receipts or Payments from this building and is also last in the Block.

- **Government Official are standing in Queue to give Daan in Daanpatra-1**

Last Year Ashirwad taken Deposit Window (D)	Current year Ashirwad Deposit Window (R)	Next year Ashirwad Deposit Window (T)/Pre-paid receipt/Adv.receipt

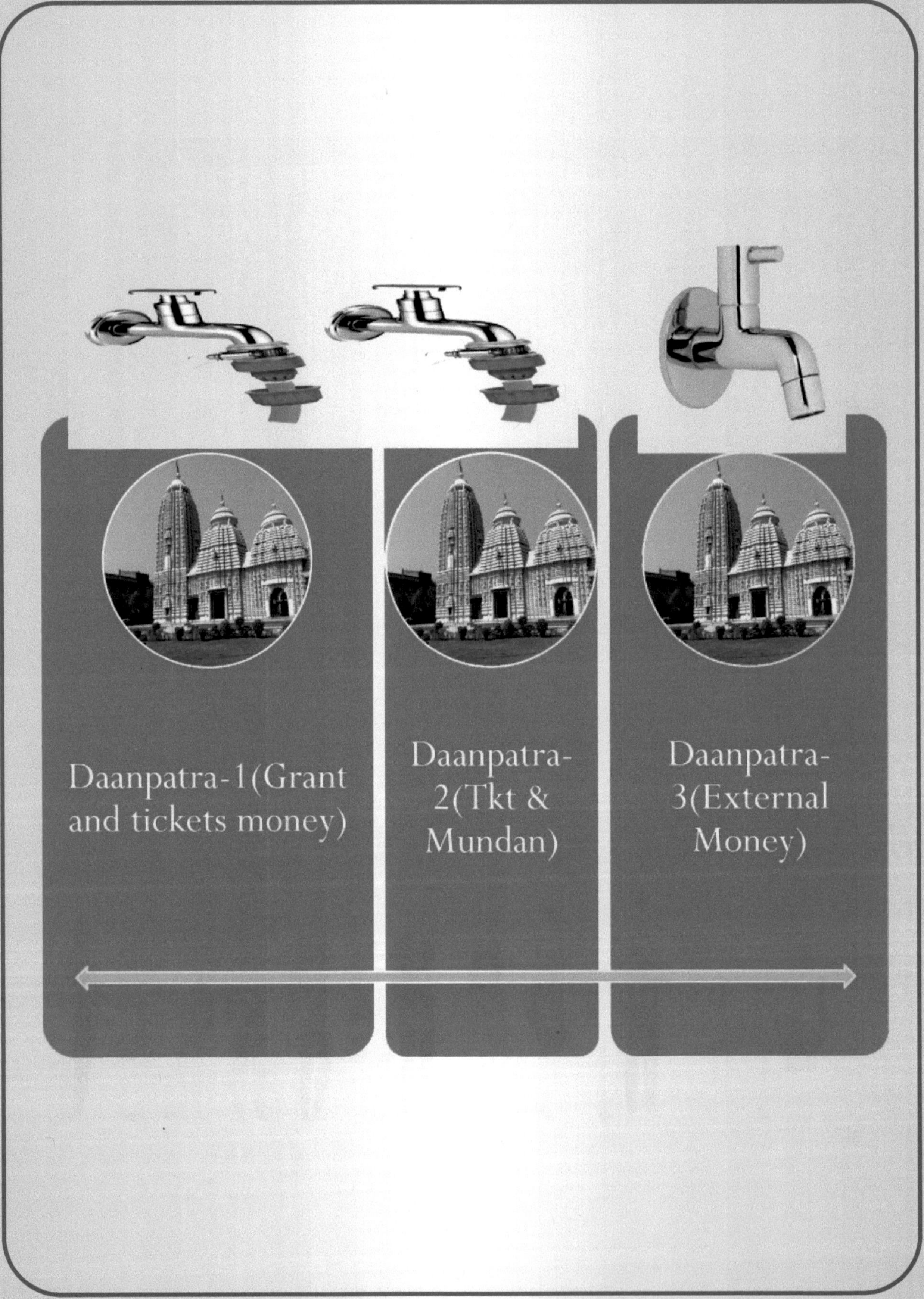
Daanpatra-1(Grant and tickets money)
Daanpatra-2(Tkt & Mundan)
Daanpatra-3(External Money)

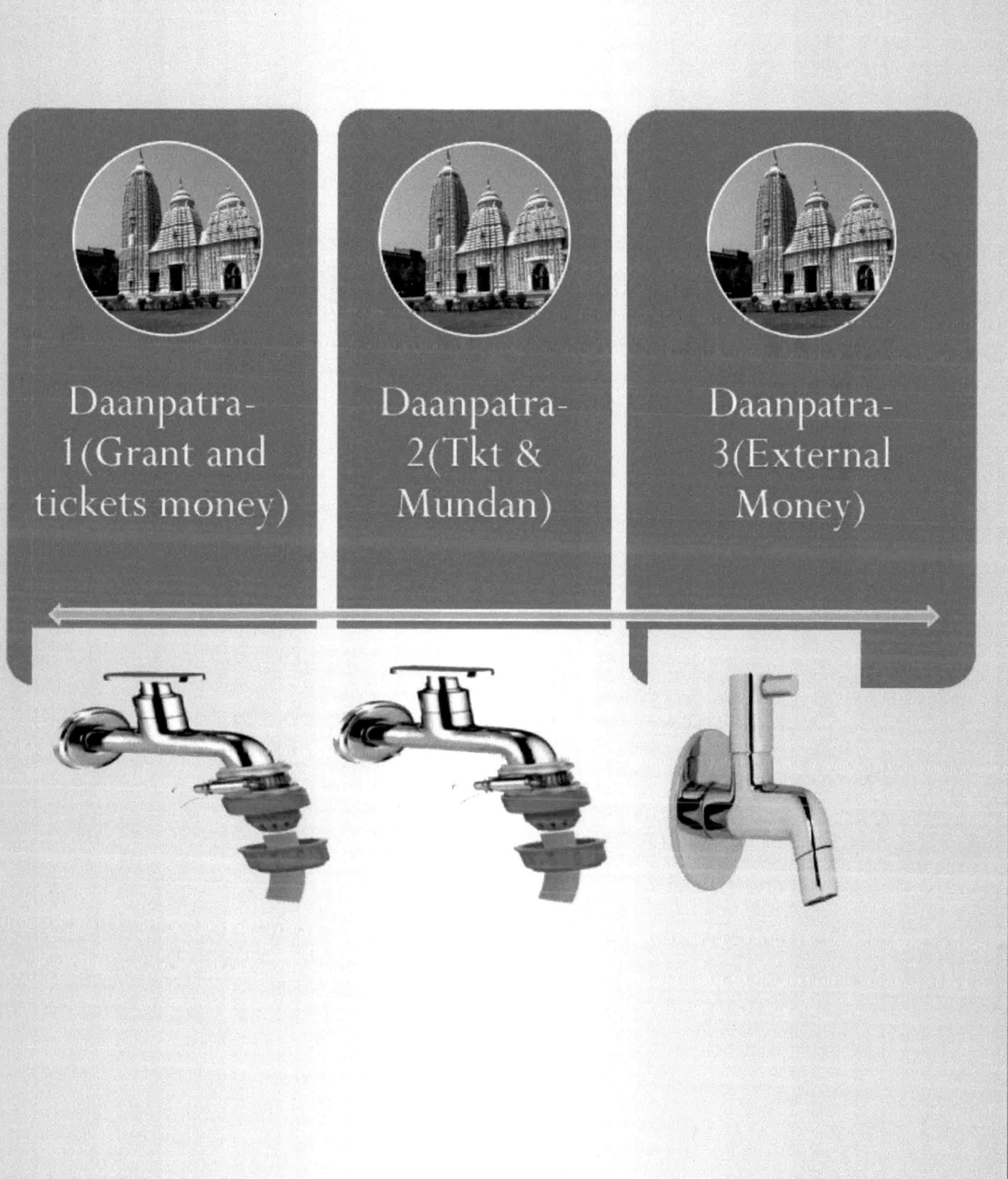
Daanpatra-
1(Grant and
tickets money)
Daanpatra-
2(Tkt &
Mundan)
Daanpatra-
3(External
Money)

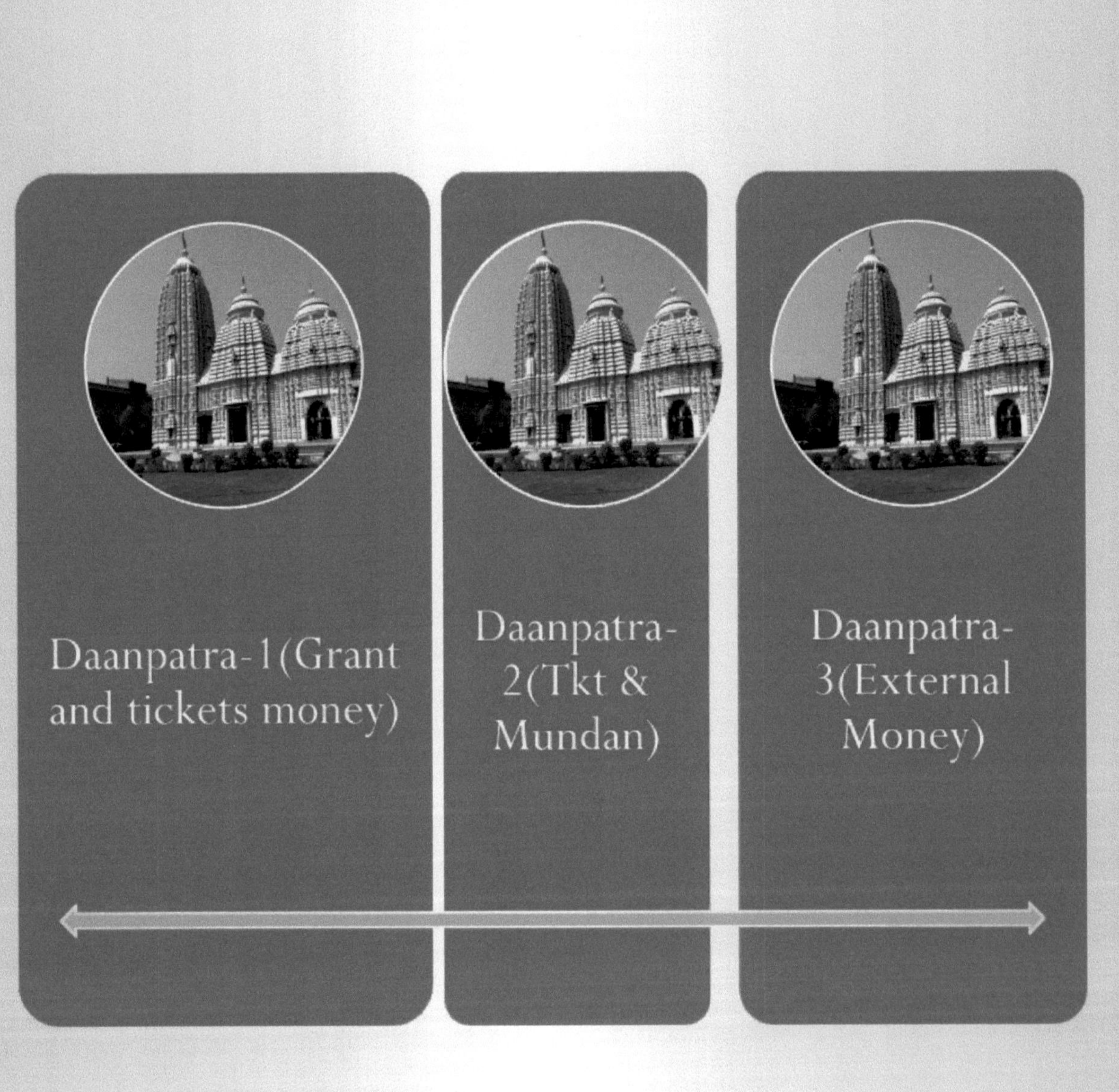
Daanpatra-1(Grant and tickets money)
Daanpatra-2(Tkt & Mundan)
Daanpatra-3(External Money)

- Block-A (Revenuc Block):- Building No.14,13,12,11,10,9 and N.
- Block-B (Capital Block):- Building No. 8,7,6,5,2,1 and N.

8 7 6 5 2 1 N
14 13 12 11 10 9 N

Accrued Income ('I') Window	Outstanding Expenditure Window ('O')

Money comes-in Daanpatra and goes-out for payments

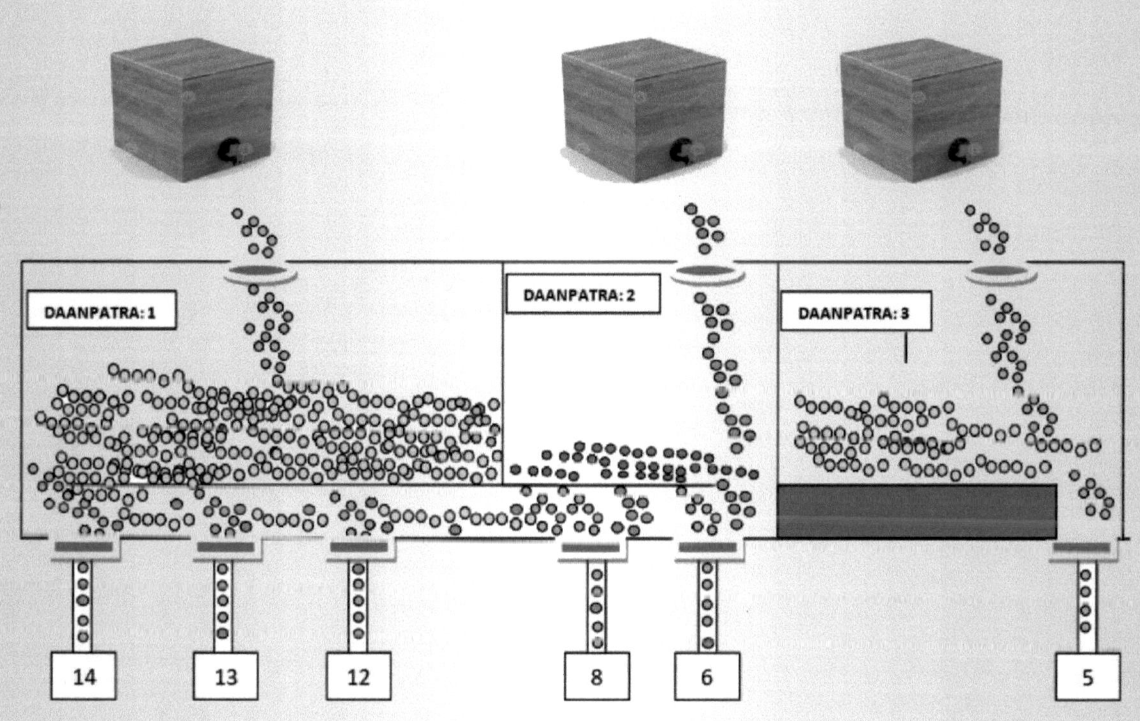

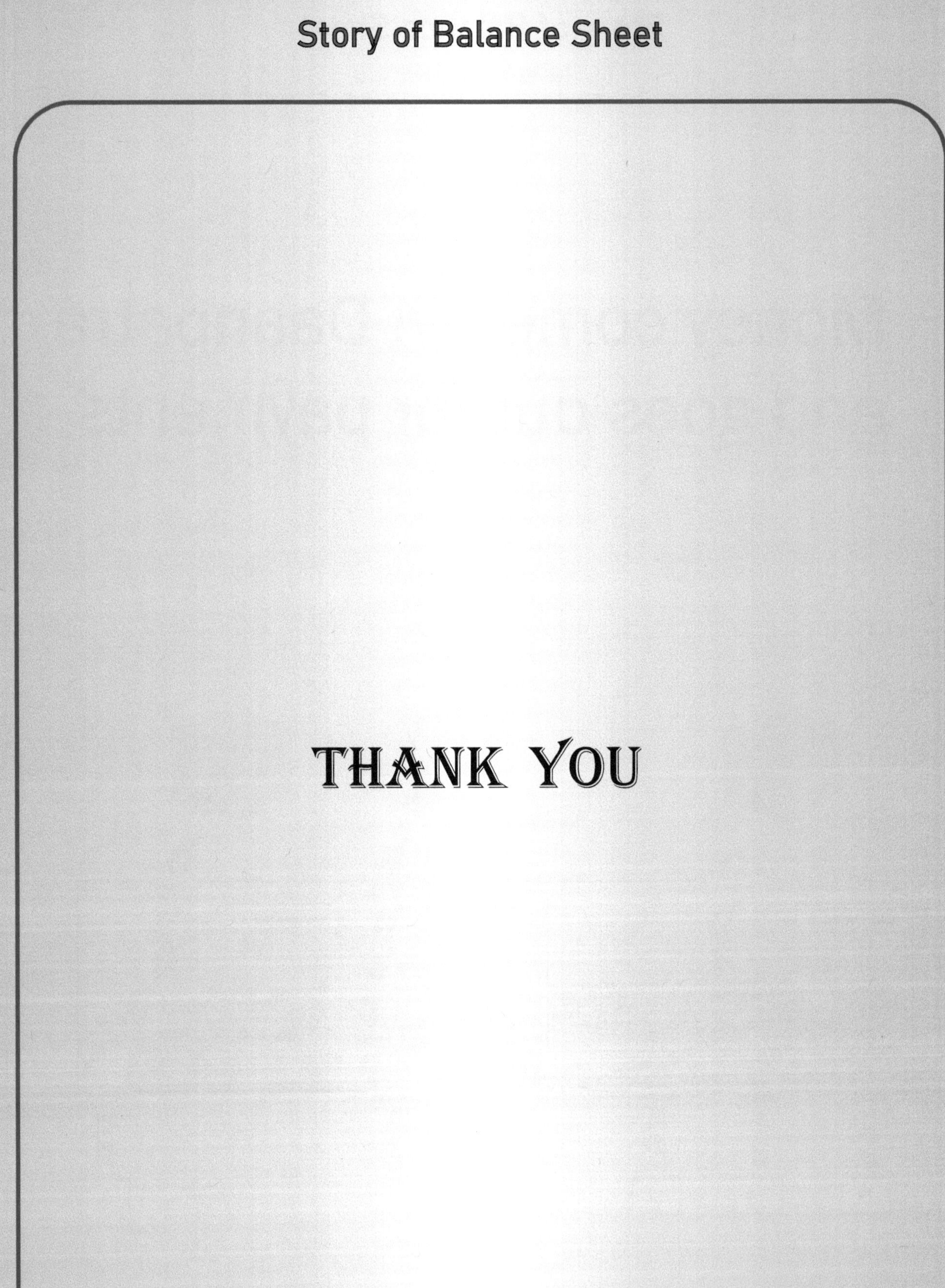
THANK YOU

9 798890 66021

Printed by Libri Plureos GmbH in Hamburg,
Germany